THE USBORNE BOOK OF
JUGGLING

Clive Gifford

Designed by Ian McNee. Illustrated by Chris Chaisty
Photographs by Ray Moller, Kim Taylor and Howard Allman
Series editor: Cheryl Evans
Juggling consultants: Tony Webber and Ross Patterson

Usborne would like to thank the following for their help with this
book: Laurie Lea, (advice and equipment) Johnny Lipsey, Jo Lipsey,
Annie Morris, Oscar Galbinski.

Contents

Juggling balls	2	Starting and stopping	18
Ready to juggle	4	Juggling with friends	20
The two ball cascade	6	Performing a routine	22
Starting the three ball cascade	8	Costumes	24
Perfecting the three ball cascade	10	Count Jugula: The vampire juggler	26
Simple tricks with three balls	12	Advanced tricks	28
Bounces and pauses	14	Juggling with props	30
One-handed juggling and cheats	16	Juggling addresses	32

Copyright © 1995 by Usborne Publishing Ltd. First published in Great Britain in 1995 by Usborne Publishing Ltd. All rights reserved. Published by Scholastic Inc., 555 Broadway, New York, NY 10012, by arrangement with Usborne Publishing Ltd.

12 11 10 9 8 7 6 5 4 3 2 1   6 7 8 9/9 0 1/0

Printed in the U.S.A.   09

First Scholastic printing, January 1996

SCHOLASTIC INC.
New York Toronto London Auckland Sydney

Juggling balls

History

Juggling has been popular for thousands of years. Historians believe that juggling was common long before then, in Ancient Greek and Egyptian times.

Archeologists have found this 2000 year old statue of a figure juggling three balls.

In the past, jugglers were usually people who moved from town to town to earn their living. In the days before newspapers, these entertainers passed on news and gossip.

In the Middle Ages, the courts of most kings and lords had a juggler who often was also the court jester, or clown. Juggling has continued to be very popular and great jugglers of more recent times, like Enrico Rastelli, Paul Cinquevalli, Bobby May and Dick Franco have invented exciting moves, tricks and routines.

You may have seen professional jugglers juggling anything from eggs to chairs; but at the beginning, it's best to learn with ordinary juggling balls or juggling bean bags.

Bean bags are often shaped like a triangle and quite soft.

They should be the same size as a small to medium apple.

Size, grip, bounce and patterns

There are four things to consider when buying balls. These are their size, grip, bounce and the pattern on them. Here are the points you need to look for.

Most places will let you try holding balls.

You should be able to squash the balls a little.

You should just be able to hold all three balls in one hand. Two balls lying up your hand should stretch from your palm to near the top of your middle finger.

The balls should feel comfortable to hold and not slippery. They should 'give' a little when you squeeze them. This will make them easier to control when juggling.

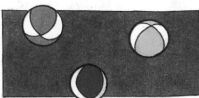

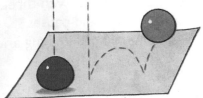

Choose bright balls that look different from each other, as they will stand out better against the background when you juggle.

For learning to juggle, it's best to have balls which don't bounce or roll away very far when they are dropped on the floor.

Making your own balls

Here's a way to make juggling balls for yourself.

What you need:
3 socks (close weave, no holes); needle and thread; filling such as pearl barley or lentils (bigger things like dried peas or beans are not as good).

Use socks from different pairs for variety.

Brighten balls up by sewing on sequins.

Outdoor filling

Dried rice, lentils and beans all swell up when wet. If you plan to juggle outdoors you will need a filling that doesn't swell. You can buy bags of small, round plastic beads or pellets from most craft shops.

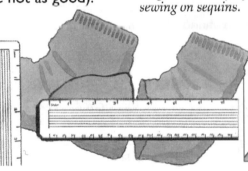

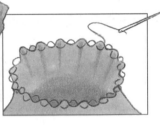

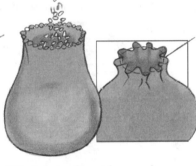

1. Measure the width of the foot of the sock. Add 1.25cm (½in). Measure this distance along the sock. Cut here using scissors.

2. Sew in running stitch around the top of the sock with strong thread. Leave 2.5cm (1in) of thread free after you've finished sewing.

3. Fill the sock with pearl barley. As it starts filling up, gently pull the thread which will draw the top of the sock together and close the hole.

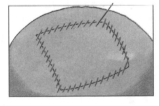

4. When the sock is almost full of pearl barley, pull the thread firmly. Keep pulling until the hole is closed as tightly as possible.

5. Cut a 4cm (1½in) square out of the remaining part of the sock and sew firmly over the hole. Repeat these steps to make the other two balls.

6. The balls each need to look different. Use patterned socks, or decorate them by dyeing, painting with fabric paint or sewing things on.

3

Ready to juggle

When you're ready to start juggling, make sure you have lots of space and don't juggle near things that could break. If you don't have much space, try to juggle over a bed at first. This stops the balls rolling away when dropped. If you juggle outdoors, make sure you have lots of space and do not juggle near roads.

Scoop throw

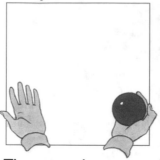 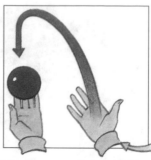 

The scoop throw is the basis of all juggling moves. To do it, hold one ball in front of you in your right hand, elbow bent.

Move your hand left across your body. Just before it reaches your navel, throw the ball up and across to your other hand.

Catch the ball in your left hand. Now, repeat the move but with your left hand throwing the ball to your right.

The flight box

As you scoop throw, watch carefully how the ball travels. It should follow the pattern of a figure of eight on its side.

To help you, imagine a box going from one hand up to the top of your head, across to above your other hand and down. Jugglers call this the flight box.

A ball from your right hand should loop gently up to the top left corner and down; from your left hand it should go to the top right corner and down.

Try to perfect the scoop throw, keeping the flight box in your mind.

The top corners are the flight peaks or imaginary points.

Try not to watch the ball all the way to your hand. Try to judge where it will land.

Showing the scoop

Pictures like these show you the pattern the balls make in the air. You can see how in the first picture, the right hand moves in before releasing the ball. You can see in the second picture, how the left hand moves in. See how high the balls travel when they are thrown.

How to stand

Wherever you stand, make sure that there is plenty of light and the view in front of you is as plain as possible.

Your hands should be in front of you and just above waist height.

Bend your elbows so your forearms are parallel to the ground.

Juggling balls must stand out from the background. Juggling near a blank wall is ideal.

Stand upright and relaxed, with your feet a little apart.

Advanced practice

Try to throw and catch the ball with your eyes closed. You are really doing well when you can throw and catch the ball with either hand three times out of five.

Keep doing this to build up a constant rhythm.

Keep on trying

Juggling isn't as hard as people think, but it does take time and work. You have to repeat some moves over and over again to master them; but you will be amazed how quickly you will be able to impress your friends.

This tricky-looking move can be learned later in the book.

The two ball cascade

   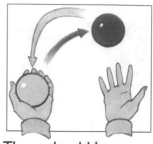

The two ball cascade is an important step in learning to juggle. The object is to make two balls swap hands smoothly by scoop throwing both. Take a ball in each hand.

Imagine your flight box (see page 4). Throw the ball in your right hand gently up and across to the corner of the flight box above your left hand.

Just as this ball reaches its peak, throw the ball in your left hand underneath the first ball, up and across to the top right hand corner of your flight box.

There should be a delay between catching the first ball and the second. Work on throwing the balls so there is a definite gap between the catches.

Getting it right

After a few attempts at the two ball cascade, think about how you throw the ball and what problems you are having. Here are some tips to help you get it right.

Do you find that you pass the second ball across your body, like the yellow ball here, instead of throwing it up?

Concentrate on pitching the second ball up to its peak.

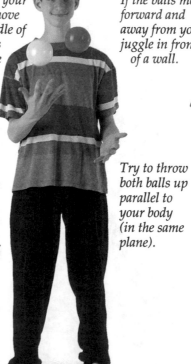

As you throw, your hand should move in to the middle of your body as shown in the middle picture.

Then your hand should move out to catch the arriving ball.

Try to be aware of this movement as it happens.

If the balls move forward and away from you, juggle in front of a wall.

Try to throw both balls up parallel to your body (in the same plane).

Advanced practice

Try doing the two ball cascade throwing the ball in your left hand first. Within a short time you will find it as easy as starting with your right hand. You are doing well if you can do the move starting with either hand, nine or ten times out of ten.

Kneeling down

If you are having trouble throwing the balls to the flight peaks, try performing the same move but kneeling down.

Keep your back straight.

Don't try to catch the balls at first, just see where they land. They should land in a similar position in front of each knee. Adjust your throws until both balls do, then try to catch them instead.

These balls have landed correctly.

Counting and rhythm

As you do the two ball cascade, count in regular intervals as you juggle. This helps you build up a good rhythm.

One

Count "one" as you throw the first ball in your right hand up and across to its flight peak above the left hand.

Two

Count "two" as the first ball reaches its flight peak and throw the ball in your left hand at the same time.

Three

Count "three" as the left hand ball reaches its flight peak. You should catch the first ball in your left hand about now.

Four

Count "four" as the second ball lands in your right hand. Start throwing the balls again and counting in the same way.

Starting the three ball cascade

How to do it

This is where you start to learn 'real' juggling, with three balls. This move is the foundation of all juggling, and most juggling tricks, so it's really important to learn it thoroughly. It starts off in the same way as the two ball cascade.

1. Place two balls in your right hand and one in your left. Hold one of the right hand balls in your fingers. This is the ball you throw first.

2. Scoop throw the first ball up to the left flight peak (see page 4). As it gets there, throw the left hand ball up to the right flight peak.

3. As the second ball reaches its peak, you have to catch the first ball in your left hand and throw the third ball from your right hand to the left peak.

Learning in stages

The red ball starts in the right hand. It is thrown first.

See how the red ball is thrown up and across to above the left hand.

Next, she throws the green ball from her left hand.

Then she throws the yellow ball and catches the green.

The three ball cascade is difficult, isn't it? Don't worry. Just concentrate on steps one to three at the top of the page. You can learn how to get the third ball moving gradually, like this.

1. Throw the first two balls and try to throw the third. Don't worry at first about catching any of them. Watch the third ball and adjust your throw so it follows the same path as the first ball.

2. Then, do the same again but try catching the first ball you threw in your left hand. Once you can do this, try and catch both of the first two balls, without worrying about catching the third.

8

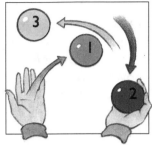   

4. As the third ball reaches its peak, throw the first ball that is now in your left hand up to the flight peak above your right hand.

5. Throw the second ball in your right hand up to the left flight peak as you catch the third ball. Then catch the first ball in your right hand.

6. As the second ball reaches its flight peak above your left hand, throw the third ball up and over to the flight peak above your right hand.

7. Catch the second and third balls and you have completed a cycle of the three ball cascade. The balls should be in the same place as at the start.

Last, she catches the yellow in the same hand as the red.

3. Next, try to catch the final ball in your left hand so you end up with two balls in your left and one ball in your right. Once you can do this well, try all seven steps at the top of the page.

Keeping your hands down

You may find that as you juggle, your hands get higher and higher. This makes it harder to juggle and will cause your arms and neck to ache. Try not to reach up to catch the balls. Ask a friend to watch you juggle and check what you do against the pictures on these pages.

Time out

You concentrate hard when you juggle and can get surprisingly tired. You achieve most when you are fresh so it's best to juggle in short bursts, 10 to 20 minutes is fine. If you do a little, often, you should soon see quite an improvement.

Focus on keeping your hands down.

Ask your friend to say if your hands are moving up.

Perfecting the three ball cascade

Once you can juggle one complete cycle of a three ball cascade, work on trying to juggle two or three cycles in a row. Count each cycle you do and aim to increase the number gradually. Keep a record of your best attempt and try to beat it each time. If you get bored, try the moves on these two pages.

Watching the balls

Following the balls is hard at first. The picture on the left shows how much is going on all at the same time. The vital move is the third ball (the green ball in this picture), so remember which one it will be before juggling. Don't watch the whole path of the balls. Instead, watch the top corners of the flight box.

Changing the height

Work on making the change in height as smooth as possible.

Aim to throw the balls up to 50cm (18in) higher than usual.

This is the first step to many exciting tricks.

Throw the balls higher than the corners of your imaginary box. The balls are harder to watch but you have much more time to catch and throw them.

Juggle the balls close to your hands. Your hands have to move faster but the balls are always in view. Vary the height from low to high and back again.

Juggle at normal height and occasionally throw one ball up a lot higher. Allow the ball to fall and just before it reaches your hand, resume your normal juggling.

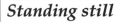

Walking

Try walking as you juggle. Keep your back straight and your eyes focussed on the top corners of your imaginary box. Move very slowly at first. Try to walk three steps forward and three steps back.

Keep looking ahead as you walk.

Make sure the floor is clear before you start.

Standing still

If you find yourself constantly having to move forward to keep juggling, try juggling close to a wall (see page 6).

Work hard at throwing the balls straight up, in line with your body.

If you still find it hard to stand still and juggle, go back to the scoop throw and two-ball cascade again.

Blind juggling

Try to juggle blindfolded. At first you may drop all the balls. Keep trying and see if you can make three or more catches in a row. The better your throws, the less you have to adjust your hands to catch them.

Blind juggling is a good test of how accurately you throw the balls.

Stand up, sit down

Place a chair in an open space. Stand just in front of it to juggle and gradually bend your knees.

Eventually you will be sitting down. Keep going until you can stand up and sit down as often as you like.

Keep your back straight and watch the balls closely.

Simple tricks with three balls

Here are a few tricks you can do with three balls. These tricks do take some time to learn but are very satisfying. Once you can do them, experiment to come up with your own new tricks.

One-over-the-top

 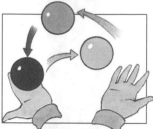 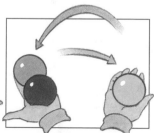

1. Start juggling a three ball cascade. Wait until a ball thrown from your left hand reaches its peak directly above your right hand.

2. Instead of throwing the ball in your right hand under the other ball, throw it in a wide arc over to the top left hand corner of the imaginary box.

3. Throw the ball already in your left hand up and right just before you catch the one-over-the-top ball. Then continue your three ball cascade.

Over the top tennis

1. Start a three ball cascade and when you're ready, perform an ordinary one-over-the-top move (above).

2. When it is time to juggle the over-the-top ball again, throw it over the top but back the other way to your starting hand.

3. Learn to do this continuously so that the over the top ball (the red ball in this picture) plays tennis, going back and forth.

You can see here how the yellow ball travels over the top of the other two. The red and green balls act as a net. Decide which ball you are going to use as the tennis ball before you start juggling. A yellow one might help to remind you of tennis.

The snatch

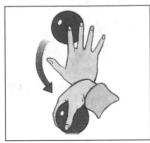 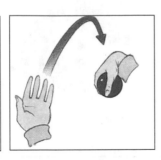  

1. Instead of catching one of the balls in the palm of your hand, turn your hand over and snatch the ball out of the air with a downward motion.

2. Throw a ball from your left hand and snatch it with your right. Try to grab it 10cm (4in) higher than if you were catching normally.

3. Don't turn your hand over to throw the ball back up into the air. Instead, flick or flip your hand up sharply to toss the ball into the air.

Work on flicking the ball up and into a three ball cascade. Over time, work toward snatching two balls in a row as shown in the picture.

Crossed arms juggling

He has just thrown the yellow ball high.

Left arm is crossed under the right.

The red ball is thrown up in the air.

Yellow ball caught.

Left hand uncrosses quickly to continue juggling.

Right hand crosses under left and throws red ball.

1. This move helps with more complex tricks later. With a ball in your left hand cross your left arm under your right and throw the ball straight up to the right hand corner of your flight box.

2. Immediately, move your left arm back into its normal position to receive the next ball in the cascade. The ball you've thrown under your arm should now land in your right hand.

3. After a while, you will be able to throw under your right arm every time you have a ball in your left hand. Once you can do this, work at doing the same move but with a ball in your right hand.

Bounces and pauses

The bounce and pause moves on these two pages look terrific and are easy to learn. They only really involve one ball as you are holding the other two as the trick is performed.

Soft and hard balls
Firm balls are best for bounces while pauses need softer balls or bags with plenty of give in them. You could make another set of juggling balls (see page 3) and put more filling inside them for bounces, or less for pauses.

Knee bounce

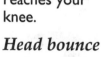

1. Let one of the balls drop past your hands and as it falls start to bring your knee up. Your upper leg should not yet be parallel with the floor as the ball reaches your knee.

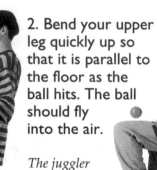

2. Bend your upper leg quickly up so that it is parallel to the floor as the ball hits. The ball should fly into the air.

The juggler keeps his back straight while bringing his knee up.

3. As the ball bounces into the air, you should have a ball in each hand so, as the bounced ball rises, you can start juggling a normal cascade again.

Try to find different ways of bouncing a ball off your body and continuing juggling.

Head bounce

1. Start a three ball cascade. When ready, throw one ball up higher than usual and slightly to you.

2. Catch the other two balls and watch the flight of the third ball. This is the ball you are going to head.

3. Tilt your head up and aim for the ball to hit you on the front part of your head just above your forehead.

4. Head the ball up into the air and continue juggling. Try to combine two of the bounces in a row.

T-shirt bounce

This is like the knee bounce except that as the ball reaches its peak, you grab your T-shirt and pull it out in front of you. As the ball hits the shirt pull it up sharply a short distance. This will bounce the ball up into the air.

Hand pause and flick start

Pauses are similar to bounces except that instead of bouncing the ball, you balance it for a while before flicking it back up and continuing juggling. Here are four steps to help you get used to this move.

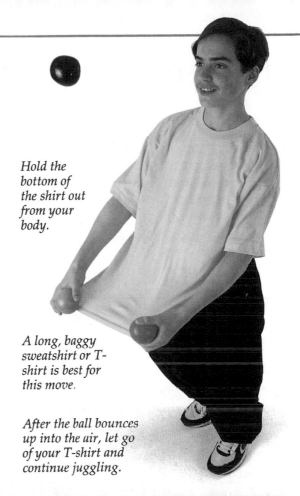

Hold the bottom of the shirt out from your body.

A long, baggy sweatshirt or T-shirt is best for this move.

After the ball bounces up into the air, let go of your T-shirt and continue juggling.

1. Hold your right hand with the palm facing down and your first and middle fingers stretched out a little.

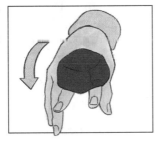

2. Throw a ball up and try to catch it on top of your fingers. Cushion it by moving your hand gently down as it lands.

3. Now, put a ball on your fingers and another in your palm. Toss up the top ball and catch as before.

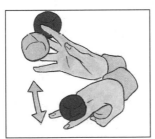

4. Next, toss both balls up with a flick of the wrist. Throw a third ball in from your left hand and juggle.

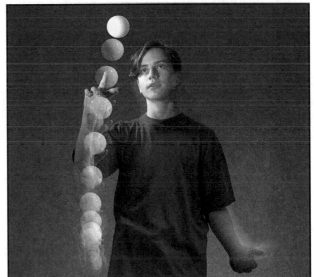

You should work on all the stages of this move. The juggler in this picture is working on step three. He is tossing the ball up off the back of his hand and trying to catch it in the same place.

15

One-handed juggling and cheats

The simpliest one-handed moves are the two ball column and shower. Learn these first, with both your left and right hands, before progressing to the four moves at the bottom of these pages. The dummy and yo-yo moves (see right) are called cheats as the juggler doesn't actually juggle one of the balls, but just pretends.

Two ball shower

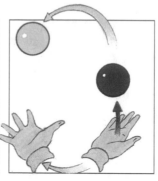

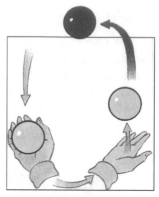

1. Hold two balls in your right hand. Throw the ball which is on your fingers up and a little distance to the left.

2. As it reaches its peak, throw the second ball in the same way. The first falls into your hand as the second peaks.

3. Keep catching the balls and throwing them in the same way. After a while you should be able to keep them circling.

Two balls to three

1. Start with one ball in your left hand and two in your right. Start doing the two ball shower with your right hand.

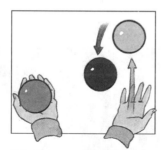

2. At some point when you have just caught one ball, scoop throw that ball up and across towards a point above your left hand.

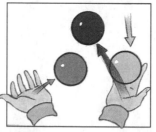

3. When it reaches its peak, throw the ball in your left hand up to the point above your right and start juggling a three ball cascade.

Three ball column

This trick keeps all the balls moving. First, perform a two ball column with one hand. Then, start to throw a third ball straight up and down in your other hand. Make sure it is thrown in time with one of the other balls. This looks good but is very easy to do.

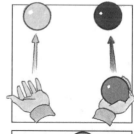

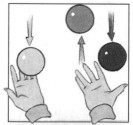

You can clearly see the column effect in this picture. To make it most effective, throw the single ball in time with the outside of the balls in the two ball column.

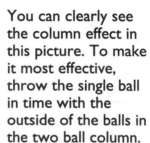

Two ball column

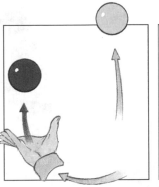
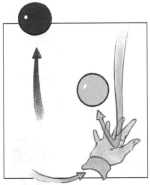
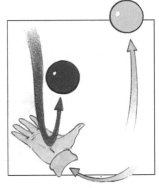

1. Hold your right hand out a little wider than normal. Throw the first ball straight up without a scooping motion.

2. As it rises, move your hand inside about 20cm (8in) and as the first ball reaches its peak, throw the second ball up straight.

3. Move your hand back to catch the first ball and throw it up straight. The balls always go up straight and never cross.

4. Time your throws to get a good rhythm. Before long, you will be able to switch between the shower and column moves.

The dummy cheat

Juggle the two ball column in your right hand. Move your left hand up and down in time with one of the balls being juggled in your right hand. Work on this so that you can do this move smoothly all of the time.

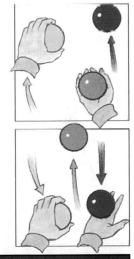

Using cheat moves

Always hold the cheat ball (the red ball here) facing the audience. Cheat moves can be funny, but only use them for as long as it takes the audience to get the joke.

The yo-yo cheat

Start by juggling a two ball column at a low height with your right hand. Hold the cheat ball a short distance above the inner of the two juggled balls. Make the cheat ball rise and fall at the same speed as the thrown ball.

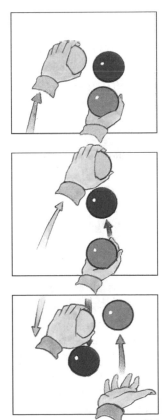

The same distance

Try hard to keep the distance between the two yo-yo balls the same. This makes them look as if the lower ball is joined to the upper one and is a good effect.

Starting and stopping

You can improve a juggling routine by adding an interesting start and finish.

Throw-in

This is a good way to recover after dropping a ball. It's also an excellent way to learn the basics of juggling with two people (see page 20). You need a friend to throw in the third ball as you juggle with the other two. She should stand about 2m (6ft) away and facing you.

The yellow ball is thrown in gently.

Get used to the speed of the throws.

He is about to throw the red ball as the yellow ball reaches him.

Your friend should continue watching.

He is now juggling normally with all three balls.

1. Your friend should throw the ball to your right hand. The ball should be thrown in a gentle loop, not too high.

2. Wait until her ball has almost reached you, then throw your right hand ball up above your left hand in the normal way.

3. Your friend's ball should reach you as the first ball you throw reaches its peak. Catch your friend's ball and juggle normally.

One handed start

One ball resting on fingers.

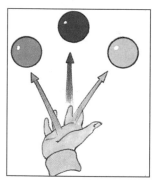

Snatch these two balls.

1. Place all three balls in your right hand, two in the palm and one balanced on your fingers. You are going to throw all three balls into the air at the same time.

2. Throw all three balls up. Don't worry about catching them at first. Try to flip the ball on your fingers up at least 30cm (12in) higher than the others.

3. Work on snatching (see page 13) the lowest two balls. Turn over your hands and throw one of the two balls up. Catch the third ball, throw it up and start juggling.

4. You need to use the snatch move to catch the falling balls quickly. Have your hands higher than usual to catch the two balls early, as shown in the picture.

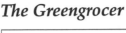

The twist finish

1. Throw one ball up high in the air. It is vital that you throw it up straight. As it starts to rise, quickly turn around on the spot. The idea is to finish your turn while the ball is still in the air.

2. As you finish, look up and watch the ball falling before catching it. With work you will quickly be able to add a stylish flourish, such as dropping to one knee as you catch the last ball.

You can also use this move in the middle of juggling. Throw one ball up high and turn around quickly. As you come back to the front, spot the ball coming down, catch it and throw up the other balls in the normal way to continue.

The Greengrocer

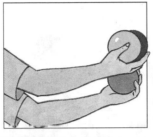 

1. This got its name because it is how greengrocers in markets often play with vegetables and fruit. Hold two balls in your right hand.

2. Raise your forearm so it is a lot higher than your elbow. Let the bottom ball in your right hand roll out and down part of your forearm.

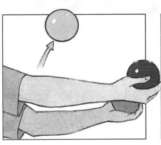 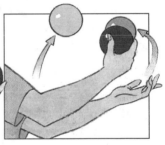

3. As it reaches the inside of your elbow snap your arm straight and push the ball off your muscle and into the air.

4. The ball starts rising up and forward into the air. Treat this ball as the first ball in a three ball cascade and start juggling.

Work on the trick by itself

A handy tip is to work on the trick by itself first before doing all the other juggling moves either side of the trick. With starting moves, for example, just work on getting the balls into the air without catching and juggling them afterwards.

Juggling with friends

Juggling can be more fun if friends are learning too. It is better to try most of the tricks shown here when both of you can already juggle some simple tricks.

Side by side

Stand next to your partner and link arms so that you stand shoulder to shoulder. Now juggle a three ball cascade with your outer arms. The one change from juggling a normal cascade is to throw the balls farther across so they peak above your partner's hand.

Three ball steal

Stand close to your partner's left as he starts juggling. When he throws up a ball from his left hand, lean across and catch that ball in your right hand. Lean farther across and use your left hand to catch the next ball which your partner throws from his right hand to his left. Collect the third ball with your right hand, bring the balls back in front of you and continue to juggle.

Stealing in line

Try stealing the balls as fast as possible. Also try different positions to steal from. One good variation is to stand directly behind your partner.

1. As he juggles, tap him on the shoulder. He should continue juggling but get into a kneeling position. Once kneeling he should throw the balls higher.

2. Lean slightly forward and steal the balls away from your partner. You step back and he should crawl around to get behind you.

3. He can now tap you on the shoulder and the whole move can be repeated. Work at completing this move as quickly and smoothly as possible.

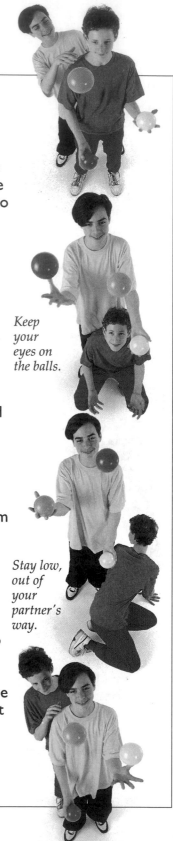

Keep your eyes on the balls.

Stay low, out of your partner's way.

Five ball pass

Passing moves are harder to do than steals. Work on the throw-in start on page 18 before attempting this pass. Stand opposite each other a short distance apart. Hold two balls in your right hand and one in your left. Your partner holds a ball in each hand. Choose one ball to be the pass ball. Both of you must remember which it is.

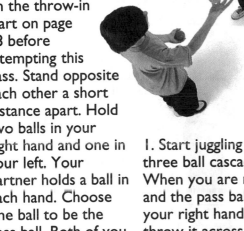

The green ball is about to be passed.

The boy in red should throw the blue ball now.

When you have just two balls, you don't juggle.

1. Start juggling a three ball cascade. When you are ready and the pass ball is in your right hand, throw it across in a gentle loop to your partner's left hand.

2. Just before the pass ball reaches your partner, he should throw the ball in his left hand up and across to the flight peak above his right hand.

3. After catching the pass ball, your partner starts juggling. When the pass ball reaches his right hand he should throw it back to you so you can start juggling again.

Six ball pass

This is the same as the five ball pass except both you and your partner switch one ball by each throwing a ball at exactly the same time. Timing is vital. You must start your three ball cascades at the same time. As the pass ball reaches your right hand, throw it straight across to your partner's left hand and continue juggling. Your partner should do the same.

Make sure both pass balls look the same.

The timing of the throws is very important.

Both jugglers must be juggling their three ball cascade at about the same speed.

Juggling tip

If you find these moves confusing, try using balloons blown up to half or a third of their normal size. This will slow the juggling down so that you can see what is happening.

Performing a routine

A routine is a selection of different tricks. The secret of a good routine is for the tricks to follow each other smoothly. It is much better to do a simple routine well than a complicated one that is full of delays and mistakes.

Decide which tricks you find easiest and work on fitting them all together. It's up to you to form your own juggling routines. Try different moves and combinations to see how they work together and make sure you have a good start and finish.

Professional jugglers often break up their juggling into little blocks. This gives them time to rest, change juggling props or tell jokes. You could try to do the same.

Short routine

1. Three balls in one hand start (page 18).
2. Normal three ball cascade (pages 8-9).
3. Bounce a ball off the knee (page 14).
4. Do three under the arm moves (page 13).

5. Repeat 2, 3 and 4 once.
6. Reverse cascade for three cycles (page 29).
7. Two ball shower, then two ball column (pages 16-17).
8. Dummy cheat then two ball shower (pages 16-17).
9. Three ball cascade with head bounce (page 14).
10. Vary cascade's height up and down (page 10).
11. Twist finish and bow (page 19).

Mirror

Work on your chosen routines in front of a mirror. It may feel odd at first but you will eventually be able to watch yourself as you juggle. Try to improve the smoothness of your juggling so that the moves all roll into one.

Showmanship

You don't have to be a brilliant juggler to perform a short routine for your family and friends. How you act as you juggle is as important as the actual juggling. Try to look relaxed. If you are nervous the audience won't enjoy it as much as if you look confident. Talking to the audience and telling jokes really improves a routine. When you talk, try to make eye-contact with each person. This makes them feel included and they may even be less critical of your performance.

If you drop all the balls

A comic expression helps you get away with it.

There's nothing you can do really if a trick goes wrong other than to make a bad joke, get the audience to throw the balls back and resume juggling. One alternative is to have a spare set of balls tucked away in your pockets. Bring them out quickly and start juggling as if nothing has happened.

This juggler is entertaining his audience with an under the leg throw in the middle of his routine.

If you drop a ball

The audience will probably think this is quite clever.

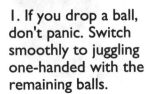

1. If you drop a ball, don't panic. Switch smoothly to juggling one-handed with the remaining balls.

2. Keeping your back as straight as possible, bend your knees and pick up the ball on the floor.

3. Once you're standing up, resume a three ball cascade until you can get back into your routine.

Costumes

These costumes are quite simple to make. They both give you a funny theme which you can improve by telling jokes.

Silent movie star

For this one, dress up like an old movie star and stay silent throughout your routine. You can even use the hat in your act (see page 30).

You can buy a bowler hat or straw boater from a joke shop.

Paint a white face, thick black eyebrows and a moustache with face paint.

White shirt with a collar.

Wear a dark suit.

A fancy waistcoat or vest makes your costume brighter.

Try to wear really baggy suit trousers.

Try to get shoes which are oversized.

Tips for a silent movie routine

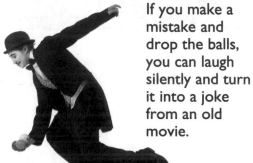

If you make a mistake and drop the balls, you can laugh silently and turn it into a joke from an old movie.

Use expressions to make people laugh.

As you bend over to pick the balls up, fall over or mime that you are kicked in the bottom.

Work on falling over in a funny way.

Your audience will be amused long enough for you to start to juggle again.

They may not even know that you made a big mistake.

Jester

A bright costume like this should inspire you to clown around.

Making the hat

You will need red, blue and yellow felt, some paper kitchen towels, a needle and strong thread.

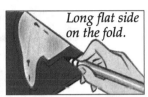

Long flat side on the fold.

Copy pattern on page 32. Pin to doubled felt. Draw around shape and cut out. Repeat for other pieces of felt.

Sew here. *Top*

Sew blue and yellow together around one arm to the top. Sew blue to the remaining yellow and red halves.

Once all the arms are sewn together, stuff the arms with paper until they stand out firmly.

You could sew small bells, bought from pet stores, onto the hat.

Baggy long-sleeved shirt worn underneath.

Belt with a large buckle.

Cut two long T-shirts in half and sew half of each together. Cut the arms off as well.

Bright leggings or tights

If you prefer, use jogging bottoms instead of tights.

Fancy slippers look great but bare feet or bright socks would do.

Playing the jester

Being a jester is all about trying to make your audience laugh. Dance around between tricks and tell terrible jokes. You could even do some acrobatics, if you know how.

Count Jugula: the vampire juggler

Dressing up as a vampire makes an unusual juggling costume. It is a strong theme with plenty of opportunities for jokes and juggling tricks.

Making the cloak

Buy about 2m (2 yards) of black lining material. Gather the middle part of one long edge to make a neck. Sew on two long strips of red lining at each end of the gathered material to tie the cloak on.

Skull balls

Make a set of balls using white socks and paint skull heads on them in black paint like the one shown in the picture below. The skull balls allow you to tell lots of old jokes such as, "I like to juggle with three of my oldest friends."

Fangs painted on your face are better than joke teeth as you may want to talk to your audience as you juggle.

The collar is a rectangle of cardboard covered in material and sewn to the cloak.

Wrap bright material around the waist to make a cummerbund.

Wear black trousers and a white shirt.

The cape shouldn't be too big otherwise it may get in the way of your juggling.

Black pointed shoes look good.

Acting the vampire

Try to look and act as frightening and evil as possible as you perform your routine.

Tell an old vampire joke to relax the audience at one point before scaring them again.

Putting on a scary laugh will also help to keep your audience amused.

Make an exciting entrance with the lights in the room switched off or dimmed.

As you finish your routine you can wrap yourself up in the cloak and bow slowly to the audience.

Garlic balls

You need to get one or more whole cloves of garlic. Choose large cloves and paint them with PVA (household) glue which is clear when it dries.

Although glue helps toughen its surface, the garlic is still quite light and delicate. To get used to juggling with it, work over a bed or other soft surface.

Store the garlic secretly. You can sew a pocket into your cape or hide it in your shirt or trouser pockets. Use it if you drop a ball or at the end of your routine.

How to use your garlic balls.

Your routine can use the fact that all vampires are afraid of garlic. Start to juggle with the garlic. Pretend you don't know what it is at first. Make faces as you recognise the garlic and end by screaming and falling to the floor or running away.

27

Advanced tricks

Juggling four balls

This looks very hard but actually isn't. The yellow and red balls are being juggled by the right hand and the green and pink balls by the left. Both hands are performing two ball showers.

At first, keep both hands a good distance apart. Once you have mastered the move, gradually bring your hands closer together. This gives the illusion of four balls being juggled in a sort of cascade.

Under leg throw

Throw one ball higher than normal. Then throw the next ball under your leg and continue juggling. The high ball gives you more time to recover.

Try at first with just one ball. Bend your leg up and throw the ball under it. The ball should travel up and across to the normal position above your catching hand.

Repeat the move until you can throw under the leg regularly.

Three ball shower

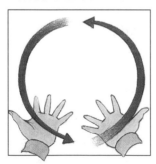

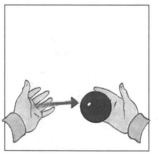

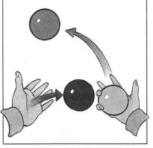

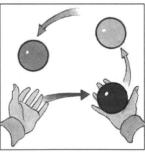

1. In a shower, the balls do not move up and under each other. Instead, they travel around in a circle between your two hands as the picture shows.

2. To do this, you must pass the balls low and flat across your chest to your catching hand. Try doing chest throws with just one ball to get used to the move.

3. Throw one of the two balls in your right hand up and over to the flight peak above your left. As it gets to its peak, throw the ball in your left hand across your chest.

4. The third ball should be thrown just before the ball from your left hand finishes its journey across your chest. It has to be thrown a little faster than normal.

Reverse cascade

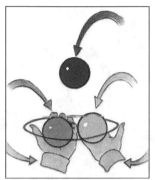

1. For this move, you need to change the way you scoop throw the balls. With a normal cascade you catch the ball and then move your hand in to throw the ball under the others.

2. With a reverse cascade you do the opposite. Your hands throw from the outside and come close together to make the catches. Note the hoop on the diagram.

3. Aim to throw the balls so that they drop through the hoop. Work on moving your hands in for the catches and out for the throws. Don't worry if it takes time to learn.

You can see in the picture above how far out the right hand starts to throw the green ball into the middle. You can also see how far the same hand has to move in to catch the red ball.

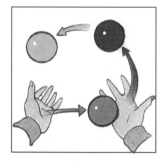

Improving your three ball shower

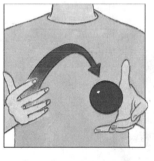

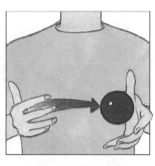

5. As the third ball reaches its peak, throw the ball in your right hand up and over as well as passing the ball in your left hand across your chest. Keep going like this.

Many people find this trick difficult. This is because you have to pass the balls in a completely different way to normal. The hardest part of the move to get used to is the chest pass. If you have trouble with the chest pass, have a look at the tip shown in the two pictures on the right.

1. Don't try to throw the ball straight across your chest. Instead, throw the ball over and a little up to your catching hand. Ths may feel more natural.

2. Over time, pass the ball across your chest with less height and more speed. After lots of attempts, you will find that the ball is flying almost flat across your chest.

Juggling with props

Any objects you use when juggling, from costumes and hats to strange juggling balls, are called props. Props can add fun and excitement to a juggling routine. Here are just a few ways to use some simple props. Try to invent your own too.

Wearing a hat

A hat, especially a hard-brimmed one, is very useful for ending a routine. You can use it to catch all three balls at once.

Another ending is to throw the last ball high, doff your hat as you bow and catch the ball in the hat unexpectedly.

You can keep a spare ball under a tight-fitting hat in case you drop a ball or want to do four ball juggling as shown on page 28.

If the hat has a soft top like a trilby, you could even catch the last ball in the hat while it is still on your head.

Juggling with your tie

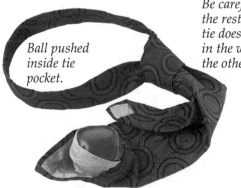

Ball pushed inside tie pocket.

Be careful that the rest of the tie does not get in the way of the other balls.

Don't throw the tie ball too high or far.

Get hold of an old necktie as long and as wide as possible. It needs to have a lining that makes a pocket in the widest end. Fit a juggling ball into the pocket and sew it securely in there.

Put the tie on. Tie it so that the wide end is as long as possible. At some point in your routine you can start juggling with the ball in the tie together with one or two ordinary juggling balls.

Everyday objects
Some jugglers use hoops, clubs, and all kinds of other things to juggle with. You can learn to juggle with everyday objects if you chose things that won't break. At first, start with things of a similar size and weight to juggling balls. Then gradually start to use things of different weights and sizes.

When you can all do this smoothly, try to add jokes.

Don't get in each other's way.

The person in the middle doesn't juggle.

Using a third person as a prop

A third person can be used in the side to side steal (see page 20). The second person steals the balls, the first moves out of the way. The third person then steals the balls and then the first person steals and starts juggling.

An even easier way to include a third person is to have them stand between you and your partner. The two of you can do passing moves (see page 21) with the passing throws going either side of the person in the middle.

Balancing props

Many jugglers perform balancing acts as they juggle. Start at first with something that is easy to balance such as a plastic cup with a flat base. Gradually work on balancing more and more difficult items and juggling harder moves. It's a good idea to balance something which you can start to juggle with at some point.

Balancing a hat on your head is fun.

Keep your head straight and juggle normally.

Don't stop here

This book contains some of the moves and tricks using juggling balls which are easier to learn. Try to invent your own tricks with your friends and never stop experimenting.
If you want to learn more, there are juggling clubs to join. Page 32 contains a list of who to contact to find out about your nearest juggling supplier or club.

Juggling addresses

Contacting people at the addresses below may help you find juggling clubs, conventions and new books and equipment near you. Remember to include a stamped, addressed envelope with your letter.

England and Wales

Butterfingers
11A Church Farm, Corston, Bath BA2 9EX.

The Catch
Moorledge Farm Cottage, Knowle Hill, Chew Magna, Bristol BS18 8TL.

Oddball Juggling
323 Upper Street, Islington, London N1 2XQ.

Tony Webber Expanding Suitcase Theatre and Circus Arts
6 Windsor Road Hebdon Bridge HX7 8LF.

Ugly Juggling Co.
73 Westgate Road, Newcastle NE1 1SG.

Scotland

Wind Things
11 Cowgatehead, Edinburgh EH1 1JY
3-5 Gibson Street, Glasgow G12 8NU.

Northern Ireland

Belfast Community Circus Centre
Crescent Arts Centre,
2-4 University Road, Belfast BT7.

Australia

Clown About Juggle Shop
PO Box 171, Cowaramup 6284, Western Australia.

Oz Juggle
PO Box 361, Northcote 3070, Victoria.

Europe (Germany)

Kaskade European Juggling Magazine
Gabi & Paul Keast Annastr. 7,
D-65197 Wiesbaden, BRD.

Jester's hat pattern

This is a half pattern for the jester's hat. Trace it as explained here, then use it as explained in the steps on page 25.

Lay a sheet of tracing paper over the pattern. Draw around the shape.

You need to draw along the top edge of the page and straight down the fold to meet the dotted lines. Use a ruler for these straight lines.

New Zealand

The Flying Kiwi
New Zealand Juggling Association
84 Studholme Street, Somerfield, Christchurch 8002.

USA & Canada

International Juggling Association
Box 218 Montague, MA 01351, USA.